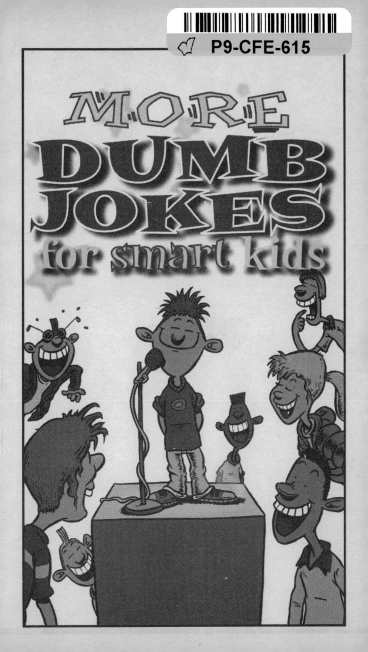

MORE DUMB JOKES for smart kids

Buster Books

Compiled and edited by Philippa Wingate
Designed by Zoe Quayle
Cover illustration by Martin Chatterton

First published in Great Britain
in 2001 by Buster Books, an imprint
of Michael O'Mara Books Limited,
9 Lion Yard, Tremadoc Road,
London SW4 7NQ

A CIP catalogue record for this book is available
from the British Library.

ISBN 1–903840–31–7

1 3 5 7 9 10 8 6 4 2

Visit our website at
www.mombooks.com

Printed and bound by Bookmarque Ltd, UK

CONTENTS

ANIMAL
GAGS

What's black and white and red all over?

A zebra with sunburn.

Two elephants walk off a cliff...

Boom! Boom!

What is the fastest thing in water?

A motor pike.

What do you get if you cross a spider with a computer?

A web page.

What's a puppy's favorite kind of pizza?

Pupperoni.

Which day do chickens hate most?

Fry-day.

Why do gorillas have big nostrils?

Because they have big fingers.

Why did the rooster cross the road?

Because it thought it was a chicken.

MOOOOO!

One evening a mother was reading a book about animals to her three-year-old son.

The mother said, "What does the cow say, Billy?"

Billy answered, "Moo!"

The mother then said, "Great! What does the cat say?"

Billy replied, "Meow."

The mother exclaimed, "Oh Billy, you're so smart! What does the frog say?"

The little three-year-old looked up at his mother with wide eyes and, in his deepest voice, replied, "Bud."

LOBSTER STORY

One day a fisherman is walking from the pier carrying two lobsters in a bucket. A game warden approaches him and asks to see his fishing license.

"I didn't catch these lobsters, they are my pets," says the fisherman. "Every day I come down to the water and whistle. These lobsters jump out and I take them for a walk."

The warden doesn't believe the fisherman and reminds him that it is illegal to fish without a license.

The fisherman replies, "If you don't believe me, then watch," and he throws the lobsters back into the water.

The warden says, "Now whistle to your lobsters and show me that they will come out of the water."

The fisherman turns to the warden and asks, "What lobsters?

MOUSE MATTERS

A group of young children were sitting in a circle with their teacher. She was going around the class asking each of them a question.

First she asked, "Davy, what noise does a cow make?"
He responded, "It goes moo."

Then she asked, "Alice, what noise does a cat make?"
Alice replied, "It goes meow."

Next she asked, "Jamie, what sound does a lamb make?"
His response was, "It goes baa."

Finally she questioned one last child, "And Jennifer, what sound does a mouse make?"
Jennifer replied, "Er, it goes... click!"

Why did the chicken
cross the playground?

To get to the other slide.

Why does a flamingo
lift up one leg?

Because if it lifted
up both legs it would
fall over.

Why do birds fly
south in the winter?

Because it's too far
to walk.

What is a polygon?

A dead parrot.

What kind of snack
do little monkeys have
with their milk?

Chocolate chimp
cookies.

What do you get
when you cross a
pig and a centipede?

Bacon and legs.

What's a cat's
favorite breakfast?

Mice Krispies.

What do whales like
to chew?

Blubber gum.

What do frogs eat with their hamburgers?

French flies.

What do cats like on their hot dogs?

Mouse-tard.

What is a little dog's favorite drink?

Pupsi-cola.

Why did Tigger jump down the toilet?

He was looking for Pooh.

What goes "Oooo, oooo, oooo?"

A cow with no lips.

Why did the whale cross the road?

To get to the other tide.

What is black and white, black and white, black and white?

A zebra caught in a revolving door.

What do dogs eat at the cinema?

Pup-corn.

I KNOW WHO YOU ARE!

A blind rabbit and a blind snake meet each other on the road one day.

The blind snake reaches out and touches the rabbit. He says, "Ah ha, you're soft and fuzzy and have floppy ears. You must be a rabbit."

The blind rabbit reaches out and touches the snake and says, "Ah ha, you're slimy, beady-eyed and low to the ground. You must be a science teacher."

HOW HIGH?

A kangaroo named Skippy kept escaping from his enclosure at the zoo. Knowing that he could hop really high, the zoo officials built a six-foot fence. However, Skippy was out of his enclosure the next morning, roaming around the zoo.

A nine-foot fence was put up. But again Skippy got out.

When the fence was twenty feet high, a camel in the next enclosure asked Skippy the kangaroo, "How much higher do you think they'll build it?"

Skippy replied, "They could build it half a mile high, but unless somebody locks the gate at night, I am going to keep getting out of my enclosure."

Why is the snail the
strongest animal?

Because he carries a
house on his back.

What did the slug
say as he slipped
down the wall?

How slime flies!

How do you know
your kitchen floor
is dirty?

Slugs leave a trail on
the floor that reads
"Clean me!"

What is the definition of a slug?

A snail with a housing problem!

What's the difference between school food and a pile of slugs?

School food comes on a plate.

What do you do when two snails have a fight?

Leave them to slug it out.

What is the difference
between an elephant
and a flea?

An elephant can have
fleas, but a flea can't
have elephants.

Why do elephants
lie down?

Because they can't lie up.

How do you know
when there's an
elephant under your bed?

Your nose touches
the ceiling.

What do you call an elephant that flies?

A jumbo jet.

What do you get if you cross an elephant and a kangaroo?

Big holes all over Australia.

How does an elephant get down from a tree?

He sits on a leaf and waits until autumn.

Why did the elephant paint himself with lots of different colors?

Because he wanted to hide in the coloring box.

21

Why were the elephants thrown out of the swimming pool?

Because they couldn't hold their trunks up.

What time is it when an elephant sits on the fence?

Time to fix the fence.

Why does an elephant wear sneakers?

So that he can sneak up on mice.

DOCTOR,
DOCTOR

Doctor, Doctor, I swallowed a bone.
Are you choking?
No, I really did!

Doctor, Doctor, I've got wind!
Can you give me something?
Yes—here's a kite.

Doctor, Doctor, how do I stop my nose from running?
Stick your foot out and trip it up!

Doctor, Doctor, I keep getting pains in my eye when I drink coffee.
Have you tried taking the spoon out of your cup?

24

Doctor, Doctor, during the week I feel like a teepee and then at the weekend I feel like a wigwam.

You're too tents.

Doctor, Doctor, my little boy has just swallowed a roll of film from his camera.

Hmmmm. Let's hope that nothing develops.

Doctor, Doctor, my son has swallowed my ballpoint pen. What should I do?

Use a pencil until I get there.

Doctor, Doctor, when I press
with my finger here... it hurts,
and here... it hurts, and here...
and here... What do you think
is wrong with me?
You have a broken finger.

Doctor, Doctor, I feel like a
pair of curtains.
**Well, pull yourself
together then.**

Doctor, Doctor, I keep thinking
I'm a dog.
**Sit on the couch and we'll
talk about it.**
But I'm not allowed up on
the couch....

Doctor, Doctor, I can't
pronounce my F's, T's and H's.
   Well, you can't say fairer
   than that then.

Doctor, Doctor, I've lost my
memory.
   When did this happen?
When did what happen?

Doctor, Doctor, I keep seeing
double.
   Please sit on the couch.
Which one?

Doctor, Doctor, I think I'm
a telephone.
   Well, take these pills and if
   they don't work, give me
   a ring!

Doctor, Doctor, I'm so ugly. What can I do about it?
Hire yourself out for Halloween parties!

Doctor, Doctor, I think I'm a bridge.
What has come over you?
Oh, two automobiles, a large truck, and a coach.

Doctor, Doctor, my wife thinks she's a duck.
You'd better bring her in to see me straightaway.
I can't do that—she's already flown south for the winter.

Doctor, Doctor, there's an invisible ghost in the waiting room.
Tell him I can't see him without an appointment.

Why are ghosts afraid?

Because they have no guts.

How do you make a milk shake?

Sneak up behind it and say "Boo!"

What did the skeleton say to her boyfriend?

I love every bone in your body.

What happened at the vampire Olympics?

All the races finished neck and neck.

Which instrument does a skeleton play?

Trombone.

Who does a vampire fall in love with?

The girl necks door.

Why did Frankenstein squash his girlfriend?

He had a crush on her.

Which happened to the mad vampire?

He went a little batty.

What's a vampire's favorite sport?

Batminton.

Why didn't the skeleton go to the party?

He had no body to go with.

What is evil and ugly and bounces?

A witch on a trampoline.

What is evil and ugly on the inside and green on the outside?

A witch dressed as a cucumber.

What was written on the hypochondriac's tombstone?

"I told you I was ill!"

What do you call a ghost mother and father?

Transparents.

When can't you bury people who live opposite a graveyard?

When they're not dead.

What is a demon's favorite T.V. sitcom?

Fiends.

Why are graveyards so noisy?

Because of all the coffin.

Where do ghosts get an education?

High sghoul.

What do you call a skeleton who won't get up in the mornings?

Lazy bones.

What is the best way to get rid of a demon?

Exorcise a lot.

Which vampire ate the three bears' porridge?

Ghouldilocks.

What sort of bands do vampires join?

Blood groups.

What roads do ghosts live on?

Dead ends.

What flavor ice cream do vampires like?

Veinilla.

What did the ghost say to her son?

"Don't spook until you are spooken to."

What do you call a wizard from outer space?

A flying sorcerer.

How can you help a starving cannibal?

Give him a hand.

Why did the wizard wear red, white, and blue suspenders?

To keep his pants up.

What was the cannibal called who ate his father's sister?

An aunt-eater.

What did the cannibal mom say to her son who was chasing a missionary?

"Stop playing with your food."

DINOSAUR
JOKES

What do you get when a dinosaur crashes his cars?

Tyrannosaurus wrecks.

What vehicle does T-Rex use to go from planet to planet?

A Dinosau

What kind of materials do dinosaurs use for the floor of their homes?

Rep Tiles.

How do you ask a dinosaur to lunch?

Tea Rex?

What should you do if you find a dinosaur in your bed?

Sleep someplace else.

What do you call a dinosaur who's been left in the rain?

A Stegosaurust

How did the dinosaur feel after he ate a pillow?

Down in the mouth.

What are prehistoric monsters called when they sleep?

Dinosnores!

What did the dinosaur say when he saw the volcano explode?

"What a lavaly day."

What do you say to a twenty-ton dinosaur wit headphones on?

Anything you want. He can't hear you.

Why did the dinosaur cross the road?

Because the chicken wasn't invented yet.

Do you know how long dinosaurs walked the planet?

Exactly the same as short dinosaurs.

What do you call a blind dinosaur?

A doyouthinkhesaurus.

Why did dinosaurs eat raw meat?

Because they didn't know how to cook.

What does a
Triceratops sit on?

It's Tricera-bottom.

What do you get
if you cross a
dinosaur with a pig?

Jurassic Pork.

What do you get if a
dinosaur sneezes?

Out of the way.

42

What is as big as a dinosaur, but weighs nothing?

It's shadow.

What followed the dinosaurs?

Their tails.

What do you get when you cross a dinosaur with a bomb?

Dinomite.

KNOCK,
KNOCK

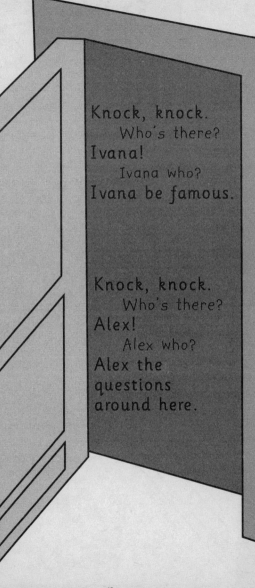

Knock, knock.
　　Who's there?
Ivana!
　　Ivana who?
Ivana be famous.

Knock, knock.
　　Who's there?
Alex!
　　Alex who?
Alex the
questions
around here.

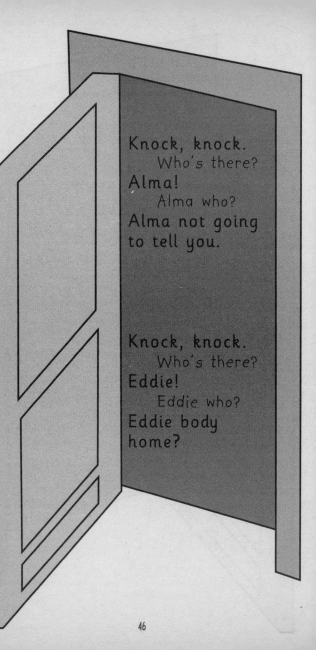

Knock, knock.
    Who's there?
Alma!
    Alma who?
Alma not going
to tell you.

Knock, knock.
    Who's there?
Eddie!
    Eddie who?
Eddie body
home?

Knock, knock.
Who's there?
Banana.
Banana who?

Knock, Knock.
Who's there?
Banana.
Banana who?

Knock, knock.
Who's there?
Orange.
Orange who?
Orange you
glad I didn't
say banana?

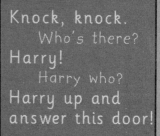

Knock, knock.
> Who's there?

Harry!
> Harry who?

Harry up and
answer this door!

Knock, knock.
> Who's there?

Bertha!
> Bertha who?

Happy
Bertha-day!

48

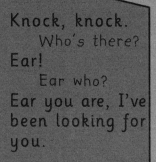

Knock, knock.
  Who's there?
Ear!
  Ear who?
Ear you are, I've
been looking for
you.

Knock, knock.
  Who's there?
Emma!
  Emma who?
Emma bit cold
out here, can
you let me in?

Knock, knock.
   Who's there?
Mickey!
   Mickey who?
Mickey is lost so
that's why I'm
knocking.

Knock, knock.
   Who's there?
Ken!
   Ken who?
Ken I come in
or do I have to
climb through
a window?

Knock, knock.
   Who's there?
Mary!
   Mary who?
Mary me,
I love you!

Knock, knock.
   Who's there?
Cynthia!
   Cynthia who?
Cynthia you
been away, I've
missed you.

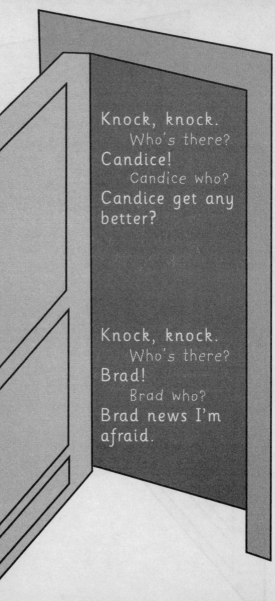

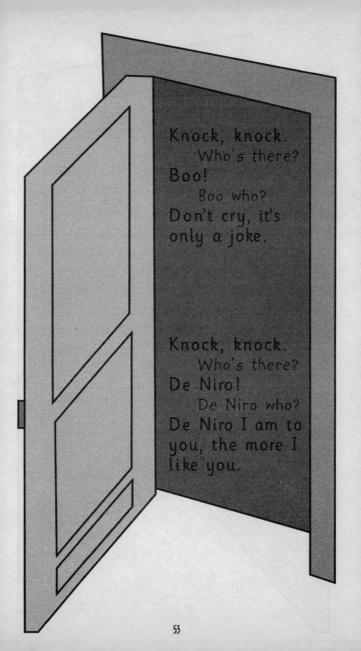

Knock, knock.
  Who's there?
Boo!
  Boo who?
Don't cry, it's
only a joke.

Knock, knock.
  Who's there?
De Niro!
  De Niro who?
De Niro I am to
you, the more I
like you.

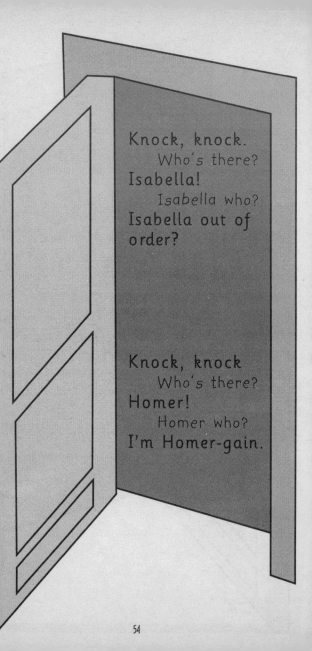

LITTLE
GREEN JOKES

PARTY, PARTY

Teenage Martian: I was at a party on Mercury last night.

His Friend: Was it any good?

Teenage Martian: No, it was really boring.

His Friend: How come?

Teenage Martian: There was no atmosphere.

CLOSE ENCOUNTER

A woman was filling her car at the gas station when she noticed a spaceship landing in front of her.

An alien stepped out of the spaceship and started to fill the craft with gas.

The woman noticed the letters "U.F.O." printed on the side of the ship.

She turned to the alien and asked, "Does U.F.O. stand for Unidentified Flying Object?"

The alien answered, "No, it stands for Unleaded Fuel Only!"

What is an astronaut's favorite meal?

Launch.

Why couldn't the astronaut land on the moon?

It was already full.

What's the best way to speak to a Martian?

Long distance.

What's a Martian's normal eyesight?

20-20-20-20-20.

What kind of ticks do you find on the moon?

Luna-ticks.

BLAST OFF!

Three men were in a conference room at NASA headquarters trying to decide the best way to spend $10 billion on space exploration.

"I think we should put our men on Mars," said the first man.

"Oh, good idea!" said the other two.

"I think we should put our men on Venus," said the second man.

"Oh, good idea!" said the other two.

"I think we should put our men on the Sun," said the third man.

"How can we do that? Won't they burn up?" asked the other two.

"No. We will go at night."

What's the best way to get straight A's?

Use a ruler.

How did the Vikings send secret messages?

By Norse code!

Pupil: My teacher was mad with me because I didn't know the location of the Rockies.

Mother: Well, next time remember where you put things!

61

What would you get if you crossed a vampire and a teacher?

Lots of blood tests.

Dad: Why aren't you doing well in history?

Kid: Because the teacher keeps asking about things that happened before I was born.

Music Teacher: What is a pizzicato?

Student: Pizza for cats.

Teacher: You should have been here at 9.00 o'clock.

Student: Why? What happened?

Teacher: What are the Great Plains?

Student: 747, Concorde, and F-16.

What kind of lighting did Noah use for the ark?

Floodlights.

Teacher: Class, we will have only half a day of school this morning.

Class: Hooray.

Teacher: We will have the other half this afternoon!

Teacher: You aren't paying attention to me. Are you having trouble hearing?

Student: No, I am having trouble listening.

Son: I can't go to school today.

Father: Why not?

Son: I don't feel so well.

Father: Where does it hurt?

Son: In school.

Teacher: Are you good at multiplication?

Student: Yes and no.

Teacher: What do you mean?

Student: Yes, I'm no good at multiplication.

Why did King Henry VIII of England have so many wives?

He liked to chop and change.

Teacher: Why is the Mississippi such an unusual river?

Student: Because it has four eyes and can't see.

Student (on the phone): My son has a bad cold and won't be able to come to school today.

School Secretary: Who is this speaking?

Student: This is my father speaking.

What did the Sheriff of Nottingham say when Robin Hood fired at him?

That was an arrow escape.

What happens when you throw a green stone in the Red Sea?

It gets wet.

1st Roman Soldier: What is the time?

2nd Roman Soldier: XX past VII.

Teacher: You missed school yesterday, didn't you?

Student: Not really.

Student: What is the best hand to write with?

Teacher: Neither – it's best to write with a pen or pencil.

Teacher: Why didn't you do your Geography homework?

Student: They world is changing every day, so I decided to wait until it settled down.

Teacher: Where is your homework?

Student: I put it in a safe place, but I forgot the combination.

Student: I can't solve this problem.

Teacher: Any five-year-old could solve this one.

Student: No wonder I can't do it, I'm almost ten.

Teacher: Did your parents help you with your homework problems?

Pupil: No, I got them all wrong by myself.

Father: How were the test questions?

Son: Easy.

Father: Then why do you look so unhappy?

Son: The questions didn't give me any trouble, just the answers.

Did you hear about the teacher who had crossed eyes?

She couldn't control her pupils.

Why does my teacher wear sunglasses?

Because I am so bright.

What kind of tree does a Math Teacher climb?

Geometry

Teacher: Name two days of the week that begin with "T".

Student: Today and tomorrow.

What came after the Stone Age?

The sausage.

What's the longest sentence?

Life imprisonment.

What's the longest word?

Smiles - because there's a mile between the first and last letter.

Teacher: Jim, be sure to go straight home.

Jim: I can't, I live around the corner.

What is worse than finding a worm in your food?

Finding half a worm.

Teacher: Where is your homework?

Student: I lost it fighting this kid who said you weren't the best teacher in the school.

What cheese is made backward?
Edam?
What did the mouse say to the webcam?
Cheese!
Did you hear about the fool who keeps going around saying "No"?
No.
Oh, so it's you!
Where does a general keep his armies?
In his sleevies.

What is green, has four legs and two trunks?

Two seasick tourists.

What did the tie say to the hat?

You go on ahead and I'll hang around.

What's red, flies, and wobbles at the same time?

A jelly copter.

What's brown and sounds like a bell?

DUNG!

74

How many rotten eggs does it take to make a stink bomb?

A phew!

Waiter, this soup tastes funny?

Then why aren't you laughing?

I want a hair cut please.

Certainly. Which one?

What's got four legs and an arm?

A happy Rottweiler.

What do you call a man who drills holes in teapots?

A potholder.

Waiter, waiter, do you serve snails?

Sit down, sir, we serve anyone.

What cake wanted to rule the world?

Attila the Bun.

What do you call a man who makes fireworks?

A head banger.

OFF THE WALL

On a wall at school someone
wrote— Is there intelligent life
on Earth?

A week later, someone else
added—Yes, but we are only
stopping to refuel.

THE THREE BEARS

"Who's been eating my
porridge," squeaked Baby Bear

"Who's been eating my
porridge," cried Mother Bear

"Burp!" said Papa Bear

STRING-A-LING

Two pieces of string meet one day on the playground. One plays on the slide, while the other plays on the swings.

They're having a great time, until one piece of string decides to go on the merry-go-round.

After a while, the string begins to feel really dizzy and falls off the merry-go-round, scraping across the tarmac, and making a tangled mess of one of its ends. Finally, it falls in a pile on the ground.

The second piece of string looks at him and sighs, "You don't do very well on the merry-go-round, do you?"

The first string looks at him and says, "I'm a frayed knot."

What lies at the bottom of the sea and whimpers?

A nervous wreck.

What do you call a person who steals pigs?

A ham burglar.

What do you call a failed lion tamer?

Claude Bottom.

What do you call an unlucky cat?

A catastrophe.

PUT THAT DOG DOWN!

A man takes his Golden Retriever to the vet.

"My dog's cross-eyed. Is there anything you can do for him?"

"Well," says the vet. "Let's take a look at him."

So he picks up the dog, and examines his eyes, then checks his teeth and ears.

Finally, the vet says, "I'm afraid I'm going to have to put the dog down."

"Oh no, Doctor! You're not going to put him down because he's cross-eyed?"

"No, because he's really heavy."

What do you call a sheep that says "Quack?"

Bilingual.

What do you call a woman crossing a river?

Bridget.

What do you call a camel with no humps?

A horse.

What do you call a small mother?

Minimom.

What do cats read in the morning?

Mewspapers.

What do you get if you cross a bridge with a car?

To the other side of the river.

What do you call a cat with no legs?

Anything you like—she won't be able to come anyway.

What do you get if you cross a kangaroo with a sweater?

A woolly jumper.

HOW MUCH IS THAT BRAIN IN THE WINDOW?

An alien walks into a shop. He tells the shop owner that he comes from Mars and wants to buy a brain for research. Pointing to a brain, the alien asks, "How much is this one?"

"Well, that one is a monkey's brain and it's $20," the owner explains.

"Okay, how much is that one?" the alien asks.

"Well, that one is a teacher's brain and it's $100," the owner explains.

"And how much is that one?" the alien asks.

"That one is a kid's brain and it is $500," the owner explains.

"Why so expensive?" the alien asks.

"Well, it's never been used!"

MONSTER MOVIES

A policeman stopped a man
who was walking along with a
monster and ordered him to
take it to the zoo at once.

The next day the policeman saw
the same man, walking along
with the same monster.

"I thought I told you to take
that monster to the zoo," said
the policeman.

"I did," said the man, "and
now I'm taking him to the
movies."

MONSTER BURP!

One day a man went to his doctor claiming that he had swallowed a monster. Nothing his doctor said would make him change his mind.

Finally the doctor gave him an anaesthetic and put him into a deep sleep. When the man woke up, the doctor was standing beside his bed. In the doctor's hands was a great big green monster.

"Nothing more to worry about," said the doctor. "We operated on you and took this monster out."

"Who are you trying to kid?" asked the man. "The monster I swallowed was a blue one."

What game to ghost mice play at parties?

Hide and Squeak!

Where do monsters go on vacation?
Death Valley.

During which age did mummies live?
The Band-Age.

Why did the monster have twins in his lunchbox?
Just incase he wanted seconds.

Monster: How much are those kittens in the window?
Pet Shop Owner: They are about $12 apiece.
Monster: Ok, I'll have a piece of the black one and a piece of the tabby.

What is the essential feature on a witch's computer?
The Spell-checker.

BIG HEAD!

This young monster came home from school one day, crying his eyes out.

"What's the matter, sweetheart?" asked his mother.

"It's the other children at school," he sobbed. "They keep teasing me and saying that I've got a big head."

"Oh, you haven't got a big head," said Mom Monster. "Just ignore them. Now, will you go to the grocery store for me? I need a bag of potatoes, ten cartons of milk, twenty loaves of bread, eight cans of baked beans, and a watermelon."

"All right, Mom" said the little monster. "Will I need a cart?"

"Oh, don't worry about that," said Mom Monster, "just put the things in your hat."

YOU MUST BE CHOKING

A man went into a cafe with a big, vicious monster on a chain.

"Sorry." said the owner. "You can't come in here with that creature. He looks dangerous. You'll have to tie him up outside."

So the man took the monster outside, and came back and ordered coffee. He was just finishing it when a lady came in and said, "Whose monster is outside?"

"Mine," said the man.

"Well, I'm sorry," the lady replied. "But my miniature poodle just killed him."

"Killed him! But how could a miniature poodle kill my great big monster?"

"She got stuck in his throat."

HOW TO CATCH A MONSTER

First, get a telescope, a matchbox, a pair of tweezers, and a very long, boring book.

Then choose a hot day and go to any place where you know big monsters live. Sit down with your supplies. After a while, you'll fall asleep, because the book is dull and the day is hot.

Soon a big monster is bound to see you and come over to investigate. He'll look over your shoulder to read the long, boring book, and he'll fall asleep too.

As soon as he does, jump up with your telescope, and look at the big, sleeping monster through the wrong end. He'll be very small. Use your tweezers to pick him up and put him in the matchbox. Voila! You've caught a big monster.

KING OF THE JUNGLE

A gorilla was walking through the jungle when he came across a deer in a clearing. The gorilla roared, "Who is the king of the jungle?"

The deer replied, "Oh, you are, sir. No question!"

The gorilla walked off pleased with himself. Soon he met a zebra drinking at a water hole.

"Who is the king of the jungle?" he roared.

"Oh, you are, sir. No question!" replied the zebra.

The gorilla walked off very pleased. Then he came across an elephant. "Who is the king of the jungle?" he roared.

Suddenly, the elephant picked up the gorilla and threw him on the ground and jumped on him.

The gorilla dragged himself up out of the dirt and said, "Okay, okay, there's no need to get mad just because you don't know the answer."

BRAVEHEART

Bill: Did I ever tell you about the time I came face to face with a very fierce gorilla?

Joe: No, what happened?

Bill: Well, I stood there, without a gun. The gorilla looked at me and snarled and roared and beat his chest. Then it came closer and closer....

Joe: What did you do?

Bill: Oh, I'd had enough, so I moved on to the next cage.

GOOD LITTLE MONSTER

Did you hear about the very well-behaved little monster?

Well, whenever he was good, his father would give him 10 cents and a pat on the head.

By the time he was 16 years old, he had $100 in the bank and his head was totally flat.

BAD MANNERS

Three monsters called Manners, Mind-Your-Own-Business and Trouble were on holiday together. One day, Trouble went missing. Manners and Mind-Your-Own-Business decided to report to the police that Trouble was missing.

When they got to the police station, Manners got frightened and decided to stay outside. Mind-Your-Own-Business went in to report their loss. The police officer asked him his name, to which the monster replied, "Mind-Your-Own-Business."

The desk sergeant crossly said, "Where's your manners?"

Mind-Your-Own-Business replied, "Outside."

On hearing such rudeness, the desk sergeant said, "Are you looking for Trouble?" to which Mind-Your-Own-Business quickly replied, "Yes, please!"

WHO'S AN UGLY BABY?

One day a waiter found a woman with a baby in her arms sitting in his cafe. She was sobbing miserably. The waiter went up to her and asked what was wrong.

"Some people were in the waiting room and they were very rude about my little boy," she cried. "They said that he was horribly ugly."

"There, there, please don't cry," said the waiter, kindly. "I'll get you a nice cup of coffee to cheer you up."

"Thank you, that would be lovely," replied the woman, wiping her eyes. "You're a very kind man."

"That's all right. Don't mention it," said the waiter. "And while I'm at it, would you like a banana for your little gorilla?"

OVER TO YOU

New jokes are being created all
the time. So we are constantly
adding to our files to make sure
we have all the best jokes
around. If you or your friends
hear any jokes that you really
like, let us know about them.
You can e-mail us at:
jokes@michaelomarabooks.com

We'll let you know if
your jokes are going
to be included
in the next book.

Thanks.